beautiful windows

stylish solutions from
HunterDouglas
window fashions

Beautiful Windows:
Stylish Solutions from Hunter Douglas

Editor: Gary McKay

Art Director: Bob Riley

Account Manager: Susan Jaeger

Contributors:

Project Editors: Angela K. Renkoski, Dan Weeks

Project Manager, Houston: Joetta Moulden

Project Manager, Austin: Helen Thompson

Writers: Jill Connors, Deb Landwehr, Liz Seymour, Steve Slack

Copy Editor: Dave Kirchner

Editorial Assistant: Barb Ruble

Photographers: Fran Brennan, Carlos Domenech, Colleen Duffley,
Susan Gilmore, Brad Simmons

Hunter Douglas Special Assistance

Carl Campbell

Charles Craddock

Donzel Garrett

David Harrison

Omar Plaisance

Meredith Integrated Marketing

President, Stephen M. Lacy

Vice President/Publishing Director, Bob Mate

Executive Director, Matt Peterson

Editor-in-Chief, Don Johnson

Meredith Corporation

Chairman and Chief Executive Officer, William T. Kerr

Chairman of The Executive Committee, E.T. Meredith III

™ A trademark of Hunter Douglas, Inc.
® A registered trademark of Hunter Douglas, Inc.
© 2001 Hunter Douglas, Inc. © 2001 Meredith Corporation.
All rights reserved. Printed in the United States of America.
Produced by Meredith Integrated Marketing,
1716 Locust Street, Des Moines, IA 50309–3023.
First Edition. Printing Number and Year: 5 4 3 2 1 05 04 03 02 01
Library of Congress Control Number: 2001132237
ISBN: 0-696-21405-9

Aluminum mini blinds, *frontispiece,* enhance a dining area. Duette® honeycomb shades, *title spread,* fit neatly inside a pair of glass doors. Provenance™ woven wood shades, *opposite,* add a sumptuous touch.

contents

a letter from

Hunter Douglas

Welcome to *Beautiful Windows!*

Hunter Douglas has been inventing and developing the latest innovations in window treatments since 1946. In the intervening 55 years, we've helped create a lot of truly stunning windows. In this book we want to share some of our most recent favorites.

At Hunter Douglas we celebrate natural light. We design our treatments to enhance light's ability to bring a special warmth and glow to your homes. Throughout *Beautiful Windows* you'll see how homeowners like yourself have dressed their windows with fashions that add style, practicality, energy efficiency, and value to their homes. And, since the treatments featured are available from Hunter Douglas, you can create similar effects in your home. It's as easy as calling your Hunter Douglas dealer.

Why Hunter Douglas? Because our blinds, shades, and shadings have been specifically developed in response to the needs of real homeowners. Since developing the first lightweight aluminum venetian blind in 1946, we have led the industry in creating benchmark products that anticipate your every window covering need. Our window fashions include Duette® honeycomb shades developed in 1985 in response to the energy crisis; Silhouette® window shadings introduced in 1991, which set a whole new standard of style and beauty; Luminette Privacy Sheers®, an ingenious combination of form and function; and most recently, Serenette® SoftFold® Shadings, which combine the luxury of fine draperies with the easy light control you've come to expect from vertical blinds. In fact, many of the fabrics used in *Beautiful Windows*—both as upholstery fabrics and to create the stunning overtreatments you'll see here—can be sourced by your window covering professional from our latest venture, *www.Tapestria.com.*

No matter what kind of house you live in, or what decorating challenges you face, no matter what window treatment needs you have, I know you'll find stylish ideas and solutions in this book.

Marvin Hopkins

President and Chief Executive Officer, Hunter Douglas Inc.

Serenette® SoftFold® Shadings enhance this living room's luxurious contemporary ambience and protect its furnishings from midsummer sun.

foreword

T. Keller Donovan, the author of this foreword, founded the New York-based design studio that bears his name in 1977. He is regularly included in lists of the country's top interior designers, and his residential design projects have been published in *Architectural Digest, House Beautiful, House & Garden, Metropolitan Home,* and *Interior Design.* Nowadays, Donovan divides his time between his New York apartment and his recently completed Miami Beach getaway, *opposite and above.* In addition to the decorating tips in this foreword, *Beautiful Windows* includes advice from Donovan in all three main chapters.

two rooms, ocean view

For 28 years, New York City has been my home, as well as the center of my interior-design business. But when it came time to choose a vacation house, I knew just what I wanted: a place in the sun. Warmth and light have always made me feel alive. Throw in an ocean view and I'm a happy guy.

I just recently found my second home in Miami Beach, which to me is a location that has it all: beaches, ocean, sunshine, and lush vegetation. I picked a unit in a new building with floor-to-ceiling sliding-glass doors and plate-glass supports for balcony railings to make the most of the wonderful tropical light. The apartment's drawbacks were few and easy to deal with: very limited space (only two main rooms), low ceilings, and no real architectural details.

I soon learned, though, that my beloved sunshine could become oppressive. I just didn't want to be awakened at dawn every day, and I certainly didn't want my favorite possessions to become bleached and dried by the sun. So I sought out Hunter Douglas window treatments, as you can too. I chose white Country Woods® wood blinds to modulate the light, with brown fabric tapes that worked with my color scheme. The wood blinds became a stand-in for architectural details in my rooms. They look both classic and contemporary, especially when mounted floor to ceiling and wall to wall as I did in my living room, *page 10*. And they are very versatile: I can pull them all the way up to savor my view or lower them and close them tightly for complete privacy as well as protection from the sun. I can slant them at any angle to let in just the amount of light I need—even turn the vanes upward to direct light onto the ceiling and bathe the whole apartment in natural light without glare.

The Country Woods® wood blinds in my bedroom, *page 15*, are identical to the ones I specified for the living room, providing a sense of flow that's important to establish in a small space like mine. To create an illusion of height and add softness in this room, I installed striped linen curtains, hung floor to ceiling.

I chose Hunter Douglas versatile, practical Palm Beach™ custom shutters with 3⅜-inch louvers for the pass-through counter between the dining area and kitchen. These shutters nicely enclose the kitchen, provide a dash of tropical architecture, and give this cookie-cutter apartment more visual texture.

I also installed off-white loop carpeting throughout the apartment, adding to the sense of flow. The walls were left white except in the bedroom, which got two coats of chocolate-brown paint. The pale carpeting and walls in the living-dining area became as refreshing and expansive as a huge canvas sail.

Even a space as tiny and generic as mine can have flair if you follow a few simple rules. For instance, find the tallest bookshelves you can, both to visually heighten the room and to organize as much potential clutter as possible. The wire shelving in my dining area holds my music system, books, and favorite objects, and provides space for a bar.

Wire shelving provides space for everything from books to a bar. A slab of plate glass makes a substantial tabletop that doesn't visually intrude on the small space. Palm Beach™ custom shutters screen a pass-through to the kitchen, add a touch of traditional Southern architecture, and complement the room's pared-down aesthetic.

For maximum crispness and graphic impact, use a two-color scheme (any color paired with white can't fail). Then add a blast of pattern, as I did with plump, circle-printed throw pillows.

Introduce fabric (such as my living-dining area's loose slipcovers and the bedroom curtains) so your rooms aren't all hard edges and flat surfaces.

Learn to edit. If a piece of furniture really doesn't fit, deep-six it. Keep only what you really need and will use. Try for an overall effect of spareness.

Fool the eye. Using the same floor covering throughout a house makes all of the rooms feel larger. A big mirror leaning against a wall—see the one I put in my living area *below*—opens up the room tremendously.

Supersize your accessories. Showcase a few bold, wonderful objects. The dramatic white star and chunky square tray on the coffee table in my living area pack lots more punch than Aunt Ida's dainty, dust-catching figurine collection.

More looks like less if it's organized. The 12 smallish ship prints over my living area's daybed would have looked fussy and ditsy if they were scattered all over. But hung in close formation, they become one big focal point that pulls the space together and balances the large window.

Remember, you don't have to go it alone. There are experts—interior designers as well as Hunter Douglas window treatment professionals—to help you achieve your goals.

Most of all, whether you do your own decorating or hire help, have fun. Putting together great-looking rooms and windows should be one of life's pleasures.

Donovan collected furniture and accessories for 15 years in the hope of finding a weekend getaway place to call his own. In this foreword, he describes how he pulled his long-anticipated vacation home together and tells you how to achieve similar effects. Though the pieces in his living-dining area represent many styles and eras, they're united by a mostly white color scheme. Brown fabric tapes on the Country Woods® wood blinds reflected in the large mirror, *below right,* echo the dark tones and clean lines of the wood-framed chairs. A single palm leaf brings the tropics indoors. The rectangular mirror acts as an additional window to visually expand and brighten the space.

—T. Keller Donovan

Rich chocolate-brown walls contrast with white wood blinds and the spreading sails of a model sloop in the bedroom. Brown tapes on the Country Woods® blinds help create the impression of height in this low-ceilinged space.

introduction

a world of windows

Windows are essential to our well-being. They connect us with nature and neighbors. They welcome the light that wakes us up in the morning and direct it as it sweeps through our rooms until dusk. They allow us to feel sheltered but not confined. They capture the sun's warmth and add architectural interest to our houses. They draw our gazes away from daily tasks and invite our imaginations to wander to far places. Windows do what foundations and roofs cannot: They invite the world into our houses and nourish our souls.

For all these reasons, at Hunter Douglas we take windows very seriously. This book is a reflection of everything we love about them. Its purpose is to show you, in as many ways as possible, the transforming quality of window treatments that are not only beautiful but practical—window treatments designed to solve specific decorating or lighting problems.

Beautiful Windows demonstrates our products' remarkable range of styles and multiplicity of functions. Here you'll see fine examples of how to use our energy-efficient Duette® honeycomb shades, which insulate against heat and cold while complementing any decor. You'll find Serenette® SoftFold® Shadings, which can stand alone elegantly or be used with more traditional curtains. And you'll learn about Brilliance® pleated shades, which can be fitted to almost any window and opened from the top as well as the bottom—a feature that helps supply light and privacy at the same time.

Beautiful Windows also shows off a few of our other innovations. These include UltraGlide™, a system with retractable cords that remain at a constant

These Duette® with Ultraglide™ shades have a retractable cord system that keeps the cord length the same—safely out of reach of children. The shades softly diffuse light in this gallery-like space. To see this space with Lightlines® mini blinds, turn to page 82.

length for easy use and increased child safety, and PowerRise®, the battery-operated system that allows you to raise, lower, and adjust your shades by convenient remote control. It's available on Silhouette® window shadings and Duette® honeycomb shades and Brilliance® pleated shades.

Throughout this book, we've pictured our treatments and innovations in a variety of real-life room settings. For example, the living room *left* shows how the translucent facings of Luminette Privacy Sheers® fit the space and decor perfectly. We hope that no matter what style of house you call home, you'll find something here resembling your own place. We've organized most of the book by architectural eras, in chapters titled "Your New House," "The Livable Ranch," and "Your Vintage House." These chapters contain everything from classic mid-century ranch styles to a 1930s Tudor cottage, from an urbane high-rise apartment to a just-built country retreat that takes its form from nearby barns.

With their translucent facings, Luminette Privacy Sheers® let the sunshine in. At the same time, their adjustable vanes allow homeowners to control light and privacy.

Beautiful Windows was written and photographed to help you find easy, attractive solutions to common challenges. These challenges might include windows that afford neighbors a complete view of your family activities, banks of glass that let in too much sun on summer days and too much cold on winter nights, and windows that allow the sun's ultraviolet rays to damage delicate fabrics. On a number of pages, you'll find decorating tips from nationally known interior designer T. Keller Donovan.

In story after story, this book discusses five needs—style, comfort, safety, privacy, and light control—that are addressed by every window treatment we produce. Our book features real houses, real challenges, real solutions, and real ideas for the way you want to live. We are pleased to present *Beautiful Windows,* crafted with pride from Hunter Douglas.

Light in this dining area is beautifully diffused by the Serenette® SoftFold® Shadings. See also *page 119.*

your new
house

From country estates to big-city spaces, today's new houses are centers of creativity, where time-honored traditions meet cutting-edge function. Their windows deserve treatments as individual as the houses themselves.

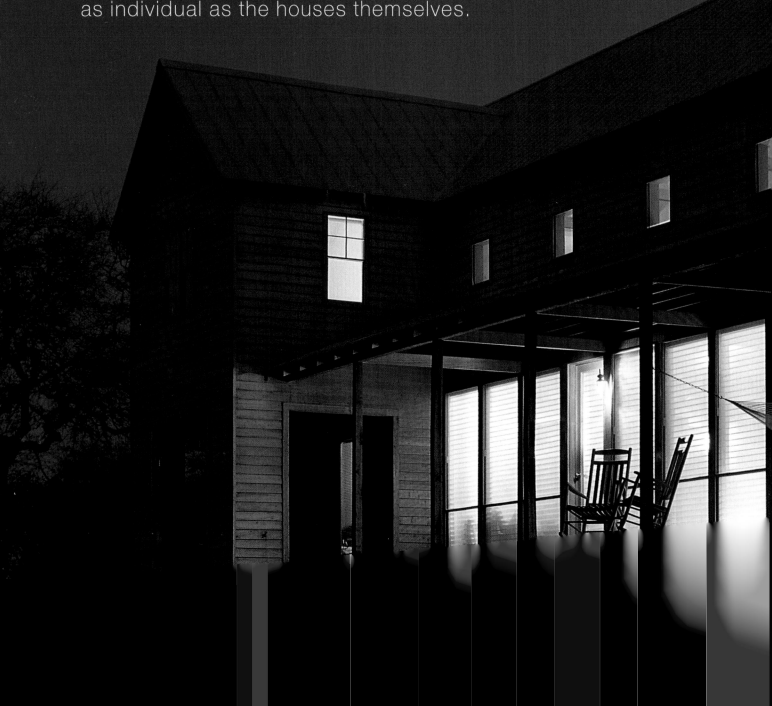

living room with a view

With its metal roof, wood construction, and wraparound porch, this weekend house owes much to rural barns and farmhouses. But it's also decidedly contemporary, with long stretches of glass overlooking expanses of open countryside. Sitting in the great room, coffee cups in hand, the homeowners spend their mornings engaged in one of their favorite pastimes: spotting deer, wild turkeys, and the occasional bald eagle through their windows.

It's no wonder this couple makes their way here every weekend they can, often with family members in tow. The house has slept up to 19 folks at a time (including several in the great room), and visitors pass the days reminiscing around the dining table the couple built or wearing out the rockers on the 800-square-foot porch. Wherever they are, they have an unsurpassed view.

The friend who designed this weekend retreat more than fulfilled the homeowners' primary goal of bringing the outdoors in. Facing almost due north, the house captures sunrises and sunsets through generous banks of side-facing windows. The Silhouette® window shadings in the atrium-style great room, *opposite and right,* create a pleasing effect. The ease with which you can raise and lower Silhouette shadings simplifies sun control—even when they're out of reach, thanks to the PowerRise® battery-powered remote-control operation. Viewed from the exterior at night, *pages 20–21,* the house becomes a virtual work of art, with the windows as panels of light illuminating the landscape.

The only problem: That view sometimes is accompanied by sun so intense it makes rooms uncomfortably warm, fades upholstery fabrics, and even casts annoying glare into visitors' eyes. For a stylishly simple solution, Silhouette® window shadings were installed all around the 24-by-36-foot great room and on the upper windows as well.

The Silhouette shadings make it easy to temper sun and heat; they are raised and lowered completely as the sun meanders through the house during the day. And after sunset? They're raised again, providing an unobstructed view of the evening landscape and the open sky. "When we sleep in the great room, we can watch the stars and the moon and the clouds. It's like a symphony," say the homeowners.

a house for art's sake

Duette® honeycomb shades are a popular choice in contemporary houses such as the one shown here. They complement clean-lined architecture both inside and out, control light, and provide privacy. Perhaps most important, they virtually disappear when completely open. The shades also help a house's windows—and patio doors—meld into their surrounding woodwork when closed. In any position, Duette shades allow art, furniture, and important materials such as the polished marble floors, *above and opposite,* to take center stage.

Marble floors cover the three rooms comprising most of the downstairs in this recently built residence. An open plan allows these rooms to flow easily into one another, and floor-to-ceiling windows open the interior spaces to the outdoors. The homeowner, a partner in a landscaping firm, wants to enjoy his new rooms and gaze on the four courtyards around his stucco-clad house.

A wide entry hall extends from the front of the house to the back, with double doors at each end. This hall, along with the living room, dining room, and entry, has proved to be ideal for showcasing the homeowner's collection of fine art—and protecting his artwork from the sun was paramount.

Continued on page 29

Duette® honeycomb shades in "Bisque" form a soothing backdrop for the eclectic furniture mix in this living room. They also help moderate the room temperature and keep the marble floor cool while protecting the furnishings and artwork from destructive UV rays.

"There's an awful lot of glass in this house, and much of it faces east," says interior designer Richard Holley. "The light is bright and brutal, and it's unbelievably tough on the house. It can ruin artwork and furnishings, and it creates a lot of heat. We wanted to keep the rooms cool—that was vital."

Installing Duette® shades with their honeycomb pleats moderates the strong morning sun, preserving the hallway's serene character. The shades reduce glare from the marble floors and make viewing the artwork easier on the eye.

Each day, the homeowner lowers the Duette shades in the living room to frustrate the early morning sun. They keep the marble floors cool and the room temperature comfortable. As the day progresses, shades throughout the house can be lowered or raised to provide the optimum amount of sunlight. In addition, they help protect the artwork and furnishings from sun damage.

Sunlight is much less a problem in the dining area; still, Duette shades are perfect for accentuating the restful, meditative view into a courtyard with climbing vines. At night, the expanse of windows can become a wall of cold, black glass. The shades warm the space and provide a perception of privacy and protection, creating an intimate, convivial atmosphere. Using complementary styles of window shades throughout the lower level unifies all of the rooms.

In the kitchen, *pages 30–31,* the homeowner, a native of Louisiana, loves to cook up Cajun specialties. His purely

Continued on page 33

"Bisque" Duette® honeycomb shades relax this elegant dining room with their soft pleats. A wrought-iron candelabra and skirted table add grace notes.

Function finds great form in these Brilliance® pleated shades in "London Haize." They provide a textural foil for the kitchen cabinets' sleek surfaces, and their metallic energy-conserving backing helps deflect radiant heat and fabric-fading ultraviolet light. They keep the room cool and good-looking all at once.

Cabana stripes on the shade over the Brilliance® "Light Camel" pleated shade punch up the color in this otherwise monochromatic library. Because of the southern exposure, late-afternoon light must be thwarted or the room becomes uncomfortably warm and energy costs soar.

functional kitchen—clean, spare, and orderly—also serves as a spot for informal dinners with friends. Brilliance® pleated shades on the bank of windows (in "London Haize" with a metallic energy-conserving backing) keep things cool and block a blinding reflection off the back courtyard's swimming pool. Their crisp accordion pleats bring a smart rhythm and energy to the windows.

A dark-green library just off the upstairs master suite stands in contrast to the more public spaces downstairs. Warm, cushiony, and comforting, it's where the homeowner relaxes and reads art books before bedtime. The deeply dyed chenille fabric on the L-shaped sofa is particularly susceptible to fading, so Brilliance pleated shades were installed to block UV light and help insulate the large window from excessive heat. Their "Light Camel" color is ideal for this restful room.

In the master bath, several long, narrow windows, along with a skylight, pump so much sun into the space that the homeowner feels almost as if he's bathing outdoors. Here, Duette® honeycomb shades put him in command of exactly the right measure of light and privacy any time of the day or night.

Since everyone wants to spend as little time as possible cleaning, Duette® honeycomb shades are an exceptional choice. Their fabrics were developed to resist dust, dirt, and stains, and they usually need just a light feather-dusting.

townhouse traditional

A spreading live oak outside the big windows of this living-dining room makes a pleasing backdrop by day and a dramatic focal point at night, when the tree is illuminated by strategically placed up-lights. Furnished with a collection of antiques, this room in a brand-new townhouse is traditional without

seeming stiff, eclectic yet uncluttered. Filled with leaf-screened light, this second-story space conveys country-manor comfort transported to the heart of the city.

The room's lofty perch above a busy street makes it easily visible from the sidewalk. It also gets lots of use after dark, which makes privacy an important consideration. "The homeowners needed privacy but still wanted to be able to see the trees," says interior designer Jerry Jeanmard. Handsome Provenance™ woven wood shades in a rich "Sandalwood" tone are framed in floor-to-ceiling linen curtains hung from wrought-iron rods, a pairing very much in keeping with the room's inviting take on dressed-down tradition.

Sunlight changes dramatically with the time of day and the direction of the

Old favorites that are very much back in style, Provenance™ woven wood shades embody the texture and beauty of natural wood. Used on a pair of oversize windows, *opposite and above right,* the shades are a key design element in a room full of orchestrated surfaces and hues.

compass: Cool northern light is as different from warm southern light as early morning light is from intense afternoon rays. Those differences can be controlled and enhanced with the right window treatments so the quality of natural light becomes integral to a room's decor.

enhancing a collection

If it's been accumulated over a lifetime, a collection of antiques doesn't usually "match" in the conventional sense. When they bring together a number of materials, finishes, and tones, antique furnishings—whether family heirlooms or carefully selected museum-quality pieces—are made even more beautiful by their very variety. However, there's also a risk that they can become a confusing jumble of competing colors and designs.

One of the easiest ways to tie together a disparate collection of antiques is to provide a backdrop rich in the same tones and textures. Provenance™ woven wood shades, with their one-of-a-kind beauty, are a good choice. Unobtrusive and natural, woven woods come in a range of bamboos, reeds, and grasses to complement a variety of furnishings. An added plus: Their light-filtering ability can help protect valuable antiques from the fading and drying effects of full sun.

This townhouse's living room has two dining tables: a round antique French table for intimate meals, *page 34,* and a long table that seats eight for dinner parties. Both sit near west-facing windows, which is problematic in the summer when the long, level rays of the late-afternoon sun linger well into the dinner hour. Adding Provenance™ woven wood shades to the windows' more formal dressings of olive-green linen panels cuts back on both heat and glare. The shades filter—rather than block—the sunlight that's part of the room's charm.

Traditional decor meets contemporary comfort in the townhouse's kitchen and breakfast area. The oversize metal-muntined windows have a vintage feel, cabinets sport retro knobs and pulls, and the counter is polished natural stone. Clean and unfussy, the architectural details call out for a window treatment that bridges old and new.

When awash with morning sun, the breakfast area can become uncomfortably warm and glaring. Duette® honeycomb shades in "Beach Shells" reveal the window details, and their soft translucence lets the morning sun illuminate without overwhelming. Plus, the shades' insulating properties have earned the window treatment industry's highest energy-efficiency rating so they help keep the kitchen cool even on hot summer mornings. In addition, they help muffle intrusive sounds from a bustling street nearby.

The view from the breakfast area is too pretty to sacrifice completely, which is why shades with the top-down, bottom-up option were chosen. Breakfasters in their robes can enjoy the privacy and light- and heat-controlling features of the honeycomb shades while still taking in a view of the trees.

Popular Duette® honeycomb shades come in a range of colors, fabrics, and room-darkening options. The neutral "Beach Shells" color chosen here enhances the sunny color scheme of warm beige and glossy white.

crisp and contemporary

Environmentally sensitive homeowners built this contemporary house on a wooded half-acre in the midst of a big city, saving several century-old oaks in the process. A dramatic 24-foot-tall window wall affords views of the surrounding trees and glittering city skyline.

Adding Serenette® SoftFold® Shadings creates even more drama and fits with the homeowners' desire for

Serenette® SoftFold® Shadings in "Straw" continue the soothing neutral color scheme the homeowners requested in this 4,700-square-foot contemporary house. Since the house is shaded by several century-old live oaks, the owners wanted to be able to admit as much light as possible yet retain the flexibility to create privacy on demand.

sleek, minimalist furnishings. The shadings also are practical, deflecting some of the city's daytime glare. In the late afternoon, they keep the sun away from a 60-inch television screen that resides in a media wall opposite the windows.

The shadings also create a unifying design element throughout the house, lending the interiors visual rhythm. Strong horizontal statements dominate in the dining room, beginning with primitive maple planks on the floor, deliberately chosen because of their exposed knots and other "imperfections." The shadings' soaring vertical louvers are a nice balance, providing visual exclamation points. These window treatments fit the house's sophisticated design perfectly, complementing a handcrafted aluminum, wood and glass dining table, chrome and leather chairs, and Italian glass lighting fixtures.

The Serenette® SoftFold® Shadings unify the kitchen, *right,* with the nearby dining room, *opposite.* A soft glow of light is achieved when the louvers are fully closed so the homeowners can create a warm ambience for dining and entertaining.

One of the homeowners is a gourmet cook and wanted an efficient streamlined kitchen. Limestone countertops, a commercial range, and tall windows for flooding the task areas with natural light are all part of this room's winning formula. The Serenette® SoftFold® Shadings help diffuse the intense sunlight, which streams in from the south during the winter months.

The windows' utilitarian metal frames dictated the contemporary touches found throughout this diminutive apartment. The generous folds of Vignette® window shadings convey a sense of permanence at the windows, perfectly suiting the masculine mood in evidence here. Their beauty beckons from the entry, *opposite*.

enjoying the high life

The resident of this apartment lives grandly in his small quarters. Situated near the top of a high rise in a major city, the apartment was designed with a welcoming entry, living-dining area, and bedroom area that doubles as additional living and working space. (The 6-foot, 4-inch homeowner professes to be perfectly comfortable using an elegant French daybed for nighttime slumber.)

A coved ceiling in the entry sets a grand tone for the larger space beyond, which has been brightened with a bleached parquet floor and a light palette on the walls. Entering guests exclaim over the breathtaking cityscape, framed by glass doors

purposely left unadorned. The dramatic view is the apartment's focal point, especially at night. Boxing in the windows helped define the room's spaces and created shelves for books, magazines, and display. Plus, it gave the windows added depth and drew even more attention to the view.

The range of colors and subtle weaves available in Vignette® window shadings gave the interior designer of this apartment a wide latitude. Here and on *pages 44–45,* he used a neutral shade in a nubby linen that adds texture. When the shades are down, the color blends the windows into the walls, making the rooms feel more spacious. Vignette shadings come with an optional fabric-covered headrail that conceals the shading when raised, leaving an unobstructed view. Their clean lines bring a neutral, unfussy character to the windows. The shadings also can be precisely lowered, a boon for this homeowner: He likes to rise early and sometimes needs to screen out an overbearing early-morning sun while he eats breakfast. A continuous-cord loop ensures smooth, trouble-free operation.

turning a cubbyhole into a castle

Living large in a small space can be a challenge: I know, because I attempt it myself! The high-rise studio on these pages appears bigger than it really is—in large part because both its windows are treated the same way, with warm Vignette® window shadings. Plus, these shadings give the space a streamlined look that's an ideal counterpoint to the fearless mix of antiques.

There really isn't a lot of furniture here, but what there is serves a multitude of tasks. A gorgeous French daybed does double duty as a place to sleep or to provide extra seating for a party. The handsome round table in the middle of the living space is even more versatile, serving as a dining table, buffet server, cocktail bar, desk, or game table, depending on the need of the moment. Who says you can't have it all?
—T. Keller Donovan

Yards of a vintage printed cotton are used here to define major seating areas and frame the living area's window. They also provide soft, flowing contrast to the tailored contours of the Vignette® window shadings, an easy-to-use updated version of traditional Roman shades.

lofty ambitions

As revitalized urban areas draw Americans back downtown, people are rediscovering the benefits of living in the heart of the city. Lofts newly carved from warehouses and other commercial buildings eliminate long commutes and offer an exciting alternative to suburban housing styles.

Typically, lofts incorporate large living areas with attached bedrooms and baths to produce floor plans that might be compact in square footage yet spacious in feeling. This big-city loft in a downtown area is a model of urban living at its best. The master bedroom is decorated to emphasize the contrast between the raw concrete ceilings and exposed pipes and the soft folds of the curtains, bed skirt, and pleated ottoman. Traditional country elements, such as the wing chair, four-poster bed, and striped cushion on the open-armed bench, make this room immensely livable.

Made of sheer translucent knit fabric, Silhouette® window shadings provide privacy and enough light to keep this loft from feeling boxed in. The PowerRise® remote-control feature makes it simple to adjust even these extra-wide shadings with one touch.

One of the most delightful aspects of downtown living is the view. The skyline changes hour by hour—and sometimes second by second—as shade and sunlight play off the distinctive architecture. At night, the streets and buildings glitter with lights, and round-the-clock car and foot traffic flows around the buildings like a river around boulders.

Like many city apartments, the living spaces in this loft feature huge walls of glass to admit light and take advantage of the scene—making the choice of window treatments one of the most important design decisions this homeowner needed to make.

She chose versatile Silhouette® window shadings, which clear the big windows completely when raised, making the most of the exciting vistas. Lowered, they provide privacy and diffuse, translucent light. The "Bon Soir" room-darkening fabric blocks 70 percent of incoming light, which is perfect for sleeping and turning the space into a peaceful, personal retreat.

The loft's guest room, down a hall from the main living area, is a clean, uncluttered mix of classic country favorites, such as a hooked rug, pristine white linens, and flowers in a bedside pitcher. The linear bed accentuates the room's high ceiling, one of the space's best architectural features, and the bedside desk and plumped-up pillows lend the room a sense of intimacy. The result is an object lesson in converting what might have been a stark space into a warm and welcoming haven.

The soft fabric vanes of Silhouette® window shadings can be tilted to provide any level of natural light. Neutral and unfussy, the shading beautifully complements this guest room's subtly patterned white bed linens.

Unlike the rest of the apartment, the guest room has but one small window, and, again, the covering of choice was Silhouette window shadings. Not only does the Silhouette shading supply continuity with the windows in the rest of the loft, but it also lets in the maximum amount of light when raised and provides privacy, light diffusion, and noise buffering when lowered. The dark frame of the window outlines the shading, turning it into a glowing focal point. In that role, it becomes another softening touch, helping to balance and domesticate the room's original function as an industrial space.

spare and worldly

A wall of handsomely proportioned windows, arranged like the panels of a Japanese shoji screen, provides the focal point in the living room of this tall stucco house in an old city neighborhood. The room's spare but inviting furnishings reflect the elegance of the high-ceilinged modern structure.

Privacy isn't a concern—the room faces a walled terrace—but light and temperature control are. Originally left bare to make the most of the terrace

view, the windows (seen from the outside, *above*) eventually proved to let in more than their share of sun and summer heat. "I like to play with the light. It changes dramatically depending on the time of day and the time of year," says homeowner and interior designer Marlys Tokerud. Brilliance® pleated shades have extra insulating and UV-blocking capacities to provide heat control and a clean, sleek look that's contemporary but still highly livable. The shades can be opened from the top, bottom, or both for a range of effects. Brilliance pleated shades soften the natural light, allowing for

Reminiscent of traditional rice-paper shades, Brilliance® pleated shades from The Versailles Collection look clean and contemporary in plain white. The living room's intriguing wall of windows lends itself to the shades' special feature: top-down and bottom-up operation. This allows windows to be covered for function in decorative ways.

greater appreciation of the detail and subtle shadings in the oval artwork.

An oversize painting injects vivid color into the sunny kitchen. White walls and a glossy black wood floor provide the clean, crisp style of an art gallery. Carefully chosen accessories and an antique faux-bamboo settee soften the edges.

In such a simple setting, sunlight can be an important design element. But you can have too much of a good thing, especially when summer temperatures soar. Also, windows that let in welcome daylight can turn into dark mirrors at night, reflecting interior lighting and exposing the space to passersby.

The round-the-clock solution is, again, Brilliance® pleated shades. Fully closed and warmly glowing by day, the shades have a sculptural beauty. Adjusted to one of their many settings, they can "paint" the room with light or provide privacy along with an outdoor view. Softer than slatted blinds, Brilliance shades dress the kitchen richly without detracting from its clean style.

The home's third-story bedroom, *pages 54–55,* gets lots of light too. Cool and inviting, the room doesn't need fussy decorations. Blue Brilliance pleated shades add another graphic element to the Mondrian-like wall of blue and white. When the shades are partially open, it's easy to enjoy the outdoors while preserving privacy.

a touch of craft, a burst of color

Two things I love about Brilliance® pleated shades—they're one of my favorite Hunter Douglas products—are that they add quiet texture to any room, and they always remind me of things Japanese: of delicate, artisan-made origami birds, folding fans, and paper lanterns. Of course, Brilliance shades aren't handmade, and they aren't at all fragile—but they evoke the beauty and refinement of Japanese crafts. They're perfect for the house on these pages, which is all about sophisticated simplicity.

As I've said elsewhere in this book, I often use the same kind and color of window treatments throughout a house, for continuity's sake. But once in a while, window treatments should add a burst of color, a punctuation mark. They certainly strike an unexpected and happy note in the bedroom of this otherwise fairly neutral-toned residence.

—*T. Keller Donovan*

Custom-made to fit the kitchen's narrow windows, Brilliance® pleated shades fit snugly and neatly inside the frames, leaving the simple wood molding—the room's only architectural trim—elegantly exposed. The shades can be opened from both top and bottom.

Blue shades help carry out a graphic blue-and-white color scheme in this bedroom. Brilliance® pleated shades come in dozens of colors, textures, and opacities to match any decor. Highly versatile, they can be fitted to almost any shape and size of window. They can also be ordered with PowerRise®, a remote-control-operated opening and closing mechanism for hard-to-reach windows.

the livable
ranch

For many baby boomers, to live in a ranch house is to return to a housing style that sheltered them in childhood. But updated expectations of privacy, energy efficiency, light control, and even safety mean that the expanses of glass in these classic American houses pose window treatment challenges. In this chapter, you'll learn how to meet them.

the past recaptured

If you grew up in the 1950s and '60s, entering a ranch house such as this 1955 brick "rambler" can feel, as Yogi Berra so memorably said, like "déjà vu all over again." The flowing spaces, long motel-like halls, ubiquitous patio, and combinations of picture windows and narrow ribbon windows tucked under the eaves typify this purely American architectural style.

"It's just like what I grew up in," says the homeowner, "but I knew I didn't want to feel like I was a kid waking up in my parents' house every morning." A single man with an eye for contemporary style, he selectively updated the kitchen, bath, and living areas; installed more dramatic lighting; and chose classic modern furnishings to transform his ranch.

This house's vast expanses of plate-glass windows also presented a design challenge. Aluminum vertical blinds in "Pearl" provide a solution that's true to the period of the house. They also add energy efficiency, privacy, and UV protection for furnishings. Finally, they diminish what is often an uninspiring view, as ranches tend to stare directly into neighbors' front and back yards.

The original owners of this ranch had changed it little since Ike was president. The kitchen's typical green vinyl flooring and countertops remained, *pages 60–61.* And the cabinets were still in good condition. Atypical furnishings, such as a chaise where most people would put a breakfast table, fit this homeowner's creative style.

A chef at a large catering firm, he sees his kitchen as a "living" space,

White Verner Panton dining chairs and an Eames table stamp the dining area with a design pedigree. "Pearl" vertical blinds, *left and page 57,* dramatically set off the grand piano and other sculptural furnishings, and enhance the modern flair of this '50s ranch.

where he can relax with a cup of coffee and friends can sprawl and chat while he's whipping up dinner. Duette® honeycomb shades perfectly fit this updated decor. TruePleat™ construction guarantees that the shades keep their marine-crisp folds.

No café curtains or frilly Priscillas for this kitchen. Because the homeowner entertains here as he cooks, the windows needed to make a slightly soft but oh-so-chic statement about style. Duette® honeycomb shades in "Cafe Candle" coordinate with the chaise, creating a cozy corner where one would usually find a breakfast table.

The rectangular windows just below the ceiling in the bedroom, *pages 62–63,* are icons of ranch style. Set high, the windows are meant to create a cooling airflow as rising warm air escapes through them. Such windows originally were left untreated, because the low lines of surrounding ranches ensured privacy. Now that nearby houses have often added second stories, treatments are essential.

Versatility makes Duette honeycomb shades a natural for the ranch's difficult window shapes; they can be configured to fit nearly any size. Those in the bedroom are opaque, blocking 99 percent of light into the bedroom. And because they draw up to stack discreetly, nothing blocks the free flow of cool, ventilating breezes when they're open.

creating curb appeal

Particularly for houses with strong architectural lines and expansive areas of glass, window treatments are much more than interior decoration. They make just as much of a design statement viewed from outside your house as they do in your rooms. Well-chosen blinds, shades, and shutters can highlight exterior architectural details and unify windows of different sizes—like the squarish kitchen windows here and the skinny bedroom windows, *pages 62–63,* all of which can be seen from the street because this ranch house occupies a corner lot.

Duette® honeycomb shades are constructed to present a soft white color outside, whatever their interior color might be. So no matter how closely you've coordinated your shades with each room's fabrics, paint, or wallpaper, you don't have to worry that your windows reveal a mismatched patchwork of color to passersby.

—*T. Keller Donovan*

Duette® honeycomb shades can be custom-ordered to fit nearly any window size, and their linear design makes them ideal for treating narrow windows such as these. Here, shades in "Cafe Candle" cover two large panes in each casement, streamlining the room's appearance when lowered. And the single, long span of shade blocks 99 percent of the early-morning light.

country comes to town

A young family took a smart approach to purchasing their first house, looking for a structure with "good bones" that they could make their own. They found it in a 1950s ranch that boasts fine hardwood floors and floor-to-ceiling windows. The ranch offered them plenty of advantages, including a convenient floor plan, large yards in front and back, and affordability.

This couple is blessed with a mom-and-mother-in-law who is an antiques dealer of some renown. With her help, they chose a

French-country theme and a classic blue-and-white color scheme to warm up the expanse of wood in their L-shaped living-dining room. Blue-and-white checked curtains draw attention to the well-proportioned windows, and coordinating colors appear in the other fabrics and in a prized collection of French plates displayed on the wall.

Though this couple's neighborhood once was quietly suburban, today it's the gateway to a district devoted to shops and restaurants. Their now-busy street puts them on constant display to passing traffic. Used more for decoration than for privacy, the curtains are seldom closed, leaving the living-dining room in full view.

Polished wood floors and a blue-and-white palette suggested the perfect window coverings for this ranch house. Country Woods® wood blinds extend the room's French-country theme and echo the colors of the checked curtains.

To remedy this situation, Country Woods® wood blinds in "Antique White" were installed across the front of the house. With their relaxed, countrified feeling, the blinds can be adjusted to let in natural light—and allow the couple to spend leisurely mornings in their robes, free of prying eyes. In the dining area, the same blinds create privacy during family meals, add to the cozy ambience, and unify the space with the living room.

A large sunroom's mustard-color brick floor and bank of glass doors overlooking the backyard were features that persuaded this young family to buy their ranch. But long summers with local temperatures topping 100 degrees meant intense sunlight made the room almost unusable several months of the year.

To temper that strong sun, Serenette® SoftFold® Shadings were selected. Made with adjustable all-fabric, teardrop-shaped louvers, Serenette shadings resemble tailored curtains, yet they can be adjusted to diffuse the light. In the heat of summer, they can be closed for complete protection from the sun. And in cooler months, they draw back for an unobstructed view of the newly landscaped backyard.

Serenette shadings offer additional money-saving and safety benefits. They keep the sun from

A vintage marble-topped table, originally made for use outdoors, was enlisted to give this dining room a country feel. The Country Woods® blinds accentuate the relaxed mood.

fading the room's toile fabrics, and they're soil- and dust-resistant—important considerations since a toddler uses the room as a play space. Also, their wand with cord tensioners keeps operating cords shortened and helps prevent children from getting caught in the cords. Most of all, Serenette shadings do what air-conditioning can't: block out the sweltering sunlight, cutting cooling costs and making this room one that can be enjoyed all year long.

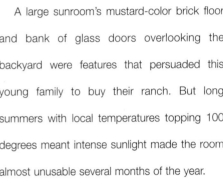

with children in mind

Serenette® SoftFold® Shadings have an important child safety benefit: Their wand with cord tensioners keeps cords shortened, which helps prevent children from becoming entangled in them. Hunter Douglas offers other innovative features that enhance the safety of our products. Our UltraGlide™ lifting system also positions cords at an out-of-reach length, and the LiteRise® touch system eliminates cords altogether. See the Product Guide for more information.

A pleated valance is made from the same fabric as the Serenette® SoftFold® Shadings, giving an elegant touch to the treatment in this sunroom. The blue border was made to match the indigo tapes used for the living-dining area's Country Woods® wood blinds. Mounted on the ceiling, the valance disguises the top of the glass doors but doesn't get in the way as they're opened and closed.

remodeled to
let the sunshine in

Two pairs of glass doors, two double-hung windows, and two skylights were added to the living room of this 1950s ranch. For a time after the improvements, the owners delighted in their sunny, south-facing space. But they soon discovered that it could be a bit *too* bright, particularly in winter when the sun is lower in the sky and rays reach deeper into the room.

Jubilance® Roman shades in "Light Cocoa" provide light control and relief from the heat in the south-facing living room of this ranch.

The couple realized that they would need window coverings that could filter the light when closed, admit solar warmth when open, and suit the room's casual, contemporary feel, whatever their position. The solution: Jubilance® Roman shades. Their pale 10-inch panels stack evenly when the shades are raised and complement the room's off-white furnishings, pickled-wood floor, and neutral area rug. Another benefit: The shades help protect the room from all that chilly glass on cold nights and overcast winter days. At last, these homeowners have the bright, sunny room they yearned for—and the luxury of basking in light they can control.

With two sets of glass doors leading to a backyard deck, the dining room, *pages 70–73,* takes full advantage of its pleasing outdoor view. But when darkness falls, the window treatments need to address

that bank of blank, black glass. In a room like this one, interior designer T. Keller Donovan recommends either elegant Luminette Privacy Sheers® that adjust for light control, sumptuous fabric shadings with a matching valance, or sleek horizontal aluminum blinds. All provide privacy, filter light, and set a beautiful backdrop for dining and entertaining. Here and on *pages 72–73,* we've shown this room with all three window treatments.

The garage-turned-home-office, *pages 80–81,* is full of creature comforts. The chair and ottoman are great for reading, brainstorming, and even power-napping. A low table can keep extra reference materials within easy reach of the desk and computer.

The previous owners had done all the hard work of converting the garage into a home office space, but they left the wall of west-facing windows bare. Tired of squinting at the computer screen in reflected sunlight and bundling up to endure winter drafts, the new owners hit on a stylish solution of 2-inch horizontal aluminum blinds. Now they find comfort with just the twist of a wand.

Continued on page 79

one dining room, three window treatments

For a light, informal mood, *opposite,* Luminette Privacy Sheers® in "Silver Mist" bring a diaphanous beauty to this room's ample glass doors. Serenette® SoftFold® Shadings in "Clove," a smoky green color, *left,* offer a more sumptuous atmosphere—especially with their matching fabric valances. The shadings' louvers rotate to control the exact amount of light that passes through. On *pages 72–73,* sleek aluminum Lightlines® "Ebony" mini blinds play up the dining room's contemporary mood. The full white curtains function as a crisp counterpoint to the blinds, which are neatly inset in the doors and flanking windows.

This dining room's focal point is a 10-by-7-foot painting by artist Sara Stites. A strong piece like this can help determine accent colors throughout a room. Decorators agree, however, that matching a painting's colors too closely actually diminishes a piece's impact and singularity. To avoid this, the bronze-toned tablecloth and Lightlines® 1-inch mini blinds in "Ebony" reflect but don't slavishly repeat hues from the painting.

Vignette® window shadings in seersucker sport a 3-inch fold and give this kitchen a nostalgic cabin feel in keeping with the narrow window style. The "Pistachio Cheesecake" hue nicely blends with the warm cypress wood tones.

Palm Beach™ Lantana™ shutters allow the master
bedroom to remain restfully dark until well after dawn,
when the sun starts pumping into this east-facing
room. The traditional yet sophisticated look of the
white shutters ideally complements the plush bed
linens, soothing palette, and pristine moldings that
make this room such an inviting retreat.

Vignette® window shadings in aquamarine "Sea Mist" suit the flowery decor of this young girl's bedroom. For utmost safety, the shadings are equipped with a special cord tensioner bracket that eliminates dangling cords, minimizing the risk of an inquisitive child or pet becoming entangled.

This soft and sweet girl's room is totally in touch with its feminine side, thanks to an artful mix of fabrics. The bed is layered in cotton, with a chambray bed skirt, dust ruffle, and chintz-draped canopy. Even the chair is slip-covered with dressmaker attention to detail.

Duette® honeycomb shades come in a variety of colors for visual interest and can be custom-made to fit special shapes such as this round, porthole-like window. They also ensure privacy—a concern here because the window faces the street—and help moderate temperatures.

But the room's three windows are enough to overwhelm the space with too-bright light and sharp shadows. The gentle folds of Vignette® window shadings provide much-needed muting as well as light control and privacy, even as they add to the feminine decor. The 4-inch fold size was chosen for its decidedly dramatic look.

shedding some light on home offices

A home office is a place where you'll want total privacy for those days—or late nights—when you feel like working in your pajamas. But you also need light control that's more flexible than what curtains can provide. Without flexible light control, there's no way to keep glare off the computer screen or out of your eyes if you're lucky enough to work near a window.

Well-chosen window coverings offer privacy, adjust to vary the light, and create a great-looking office, all at the same time. I especially like Hunter Douglas® horizontal blinds because they adjust so easily and precisely. They're also very appealing from a style standpoint: I prefer home offices that are sleeker and less fussy than other living areas. Horizontal blinds help establish a clean, up-to-date, organized look.

—*T. Keller Donovan*

The camel-color slats of these 2-inch aluminum horizontal blinds blend with the walls of this home office. Each slat rotates a full 180 degrees for total light control, and the de-Light™ feature eliminates unwanted light leaks.

the ranch reborn

This architect-designed residence was recently built as a tribute to one-story, mid-century houses: It provides an apt setting for a lovingly accumulated collection of 1950s and '60s furniture. Dressed up in a medley of melony retro colors and made contemporary with concrete floors and gallery-style lighting, the house embodies the current interest in a style now called Mid-Century Modern. This style harks back to an era of space-age design that emphasized whiplash curves, spare interiors, and materials like chrome and plastic.

The house has one major drawback: It's sited so close to the street that neighbors and passersby can peer into the big windows and French doors as they walk past. The solution—in keeping with the period of the house—was to install 1-inch Lightlines® mini blinds in silvery aluminum. Providing light control and privacy, the blinds make a practical design statement: de-Light™ hidden cord-routing holes and a generous number of slats help the blinds close to almost total darkness, and the slats are constructed of a resilient alloy unique to Hunter Douglas that bounces back when a slat is bent.

In the dining area, *pages 84–85,* vinyl-upholstered chairs are pulled up to an Eisenhower-era table. Lightlines mini blinds again were used to capture the house's air of sophisticated nostalgia without compromising its sense of open space. The blinds all but disappear when tilted fully open but create to-tal privacy when closed. More stylish than their earlier-man-ufactured counterparts, the new generation of aluminum blinds comes in an appealing range of hues and finishes.

a vogue for vintage style

There was a time when no 1940s detective movie was complete without a shot of stripes of light streaming through the slats of a venetian blind. Like martinis and swing dancing, the old-fashioned blind has been revived and is as popular as it ever was.

The origins of the venetian blind are lost, but scholars believe it was invented in Persia or Egypt as a way to filter sunlight. Venetian traders brought the adjustable slatted blind concept to Europe, where it was widely adopted. In America, paintings show venetian blinds on the windows of the hall where the Declaration of Independence was signed.

The blind entered the modern era in the '40s when Hunter Douglas invented lightweight aluminum slats and developed improved hardware. The wide-slat blind gave way to the sleek mini blind in the 1970s and '80s, and today both 1- and 2-inch blinds are back in fashion.

Lightlines® mini blinds inset in the doors in this hallway, *above,* and windows in the living room, *opposite,* keep the focus on the frames and trim, and the house's period decor.

Fun and funky, these 1-inch Lightlines® mini blinds fit right in with a collection of furniture and ceramics from the 1950s and '60s. The blinds are a bold fashion statement with a practical purpose, affording privacy and light control with the simple twist of a wand.

your vintage
house

Vintage houses boast architecture, materials, and craftsmanship now hard to find in newer structures. These houses deserve window treatments befitting details like deep sills, seasoned plank floors, and brick fireplaces. In addition to enhancing older architecture, the right window treatments can improve light control, UV-light protection, and energy efficiency.

a brighter bungalow

Living near two major art museums on a narrow, tree-lined inner-city street has its advantages. But it also means lots of foot traffic and prying eyes. Joggers can't resist slowing down to admire this classic, Craftsman-style bungalow, with its low-pitched roof and generous overhangs.

Inside, those same charming features can make for gloomy interiors. Here, the homeowner chose to update tradition, working with his interior designer to create light, bright rooms that are crisp, clean, and spare. He picked Palm Beach™ custom shutters for the living room because they attach to the windows' interior  frames and don't hide the molding detail. "I wanted to respect the architecture," he says. "What's the point of living in a house of this style if you cover up its details?" The shutters have 3⅜-inch louvers right in scale with the wide moldings.

This homeowner loves to host dinner parties, so the dining room, *page 90,* is as important as any other. The Palm Beach shutters, here in bright "White," work well with the calming, tea-leaf-green walls. Made of a washable, UV-resistant compound,

A shade tree, *above,* **frames the living room's view of the front yard. Shutters,** *left and pages 86–87,* **open to draw in daylight but can be closed during weekends when sidewalk traffic becomes a bit too nosy.**

While filtering light in the dining room, Palm Beach™ custom shutters from Hunter Douglas also flatter the period architecture. Here the room's designer chose Hunter Douglas "White" color to match the woodwork.

they won't crack, chip, or warp. They also lend continuity to the adjoining living room, making for a great first impression.

Many Craftsman-style houses have an attached sunroom. The homeowner uses his as a second, more intimate living space, pairing two Duncan Phyfe-style sofas with a glass-topped coffee table. Silhouette® window shadings have a soft, sheer, refined personality that pairs nicely with the sofas' pale upholstery. The shadings adjust to admit as much light and solar warmth as desired.

Silhouette® window shadings in "Fresh Lotus" add to this sunroom's tranquil ambience. Their 3-inch vanes tilt easily to provide precise light control and keep damaging ultraviolet light from harming the floor covering and upholstery fabrics.

georgian graces

Georgian architecture, with its pleasing symmetry and classical references, has always connoted comfort and generosity. This homeowner takes the style of her 1930s Georgian to a high level of tailored luxury. An interior designer, she's known for creating rooms that are dressy yet welcoming.

The landing shown here, which is perched at the top of a central staircase, opens onto three bedrooms. The homeowner designed the space, with its alcove and built-in sun-splashed window seat, specifically as a place to talk on the telephone— to conduct a bit of business or have leisurely chats with far-off family members.

Given her desire to make every detail of her house as accommodating as possible, she placed a table with pens and a notebook by the window seat. The seat is further equipped with an overstuffed cushion and four plush pillows that invite one to stretch out and relax.

Country Woods® wood blinds with 2-inch horizontal slats provide complete light control here, allowing everything from warming sunshine to an indirect glow to cooling shade. The blinds' "Linen" color complements the rich fabrics on the shade, pillows, and the panels inside the doors of the corner cabinets; vertical tapes provide a dressmaker's detail. The round window near the alcove's peak is left untreated, both to show off its mullions and to allow the homeowner to watch the sun's rays sweep across her walls.

In this landing's inviting window alcove, Country Woods® wood blinds in a "Linen" color provide flexible light control. They also coordinate perfectly with the striped, tasseled fabric shade they accompany.

With its overstuffed love seat and chair, abundance of pillows, and a fringed throw, this sitting area in the master bedroom exemplifies comfort and luxury. The bedroom is designed to create an inviting adult getaway, a place where, at the end of the day, the homeowner and her husband can shut the door and feel as though they're experiencing all the pampering amenities of a four-star hotel.

Because the homeowner loves the softness that layered window treatments bring to a room, she combined Vignette® window shadings with lined curtains. The "French Vanilla" seersucker shadings provide daytime privacy and a calming glow when lowered, and a full-window view when fully raised. At night, the closed curtains envelop the bedroom in a velvety darkness that thwarts early-morning sun. The sitting area faces a high four-poster bed, *pages 96–97,* which is flanked by windows treated with an identical combination of Vignette window shadings, curtains, and rods.

Four-inch-fold Vignette® window shadings in "French Vanilla" seersucker offer privacy and light control. The treatments' low-key elegance complements this traditionally furnished sitting area.

To enhance the sumptuous feeling of their bedroom, the owners added on a new bathroom, *pages 98–99,* complete with a deep soaking tub. This room provides an excellent opportunity to combine two Hunter Douglas treatments. Easy-care Palm Beach™ Lantana™ shutters on the

windows' lower portions provide absolute privacy while filtering daylight. Easy to clean and impervious to the occasional splash of water, they're perfect for this application. Installed above the shutters, Vignette® window shadings provide continuity with the adjoining bedroom and, when fully raised, allow for a view of the sky and clouds during a calming soak on a sunny afternoon. Combined with the bath's sitting area, the fabric Vignette window shadings also take the edge off the room's hard surfaces.

Vignette® shadings in "French Vanilla" cover a pair of windows in this master suite. Curtains and pillows pick up the color of the shadings' narrow, subtle stripe. The shadings are identical to those in the suite's sitting area and on top of the Palm Beach™ Lantana™ shutters in the bath sitting area, *above,* and the bath.

Continued on page 100

Palm Beach™ Lantana™ shutters add architectural detail to the bottom half of the window wall in this tiled master bath. Made of a composite material, the shutters are impervious to warping and cracking. This means they're ideal for the extra-humid environment of a bathroom. Vignette® window shadings above the shutters match those in the master bedroom and add a soft dimension to the bath.

The boy's bedroom exhibits several characteristic Georgian-style, 1930s-era details: ample proportions, higher-than-average ceilings, handsome crown and base moldings, and original oak floors. Antique furniture is a fitting complement to the room's classic architecture: The homeowner's challenge lay in finding pieces that were stylish without being perceived as fussy by her sports-minded young son. The eclectic mix she finally selected includes an early-1900s French faux-bamboo double bed and a small-scale 1920s English desk, complete with a leather top.

Country Woods® 2-inch wood blinds in rustic "Warm Cherry" provide privacy and light control in this young boy's bedroom. Almond tapes add a pleasing, light contrast to the wood; awning-striped curtains complete the look.

Honoring the style and finish of the room's antique pieces was a primary consideration when choosing the window coverings. It was a given that the room needed complete privacy and light control (what kid doesn't love sleeping a little late on weekends?). Country Woods® wood blinds were the perfect choice: Their "Warm Cherry" hue complements the luster of the old, well-polished furniture, and the 2-inch horizontal slat size is a design classic. Sage-and-taupe-striped curtains flanking the double windows add a completing flourish to this handsome room.

a perfect cottage for two

At one time or another, we've all fallen in love with a house like this: a 1930s Tudor-style brick charmer with a pitched roof, arched front door, and plenty of windows all around. As functional today as it was decades ago, this house offered the ideal size and floor plan for a young couple just starting out. Even better, the residence had been recently renovated. The hard work was already done, leaving its new owners with just the pleasant task

of giving it their personal decorating touches.

"Because our house is so small, we wanted furnishings that were large in scale. Those kinds of pieces would make the rooms seem full but not cluttered," says one of the homeowners. Fortunately, there are plenty of well-placed windows that also make the rooms seem larger. An interplay of taupe and white with accents of black visually unites the small spaces.

For reading, entertaining, or just lounging, the sunroom is the most popular room in the house. Animating the space are an easy-maintenance slipcovered sofa, chair, and oversize ottoman that doubles as a coffee table for trays of refreshments.

A pair of dramatic arched windows adds charm but also a particular set of problems. Facing the street and the house next door, the windows are enormous openings that put the couple and their activities on full display. The perfect solution? Brilliance® pleated shades in "Light

A pair of large brick windows is key to the character of the sunroom and the house's curb appeal. Brilliance® pleated shades filter strong daylight without covering these dramatic arches. They also permit a diffused view of the recently landscaped front and side yards.

Camel" to coordinate with the wall color. Well suited to unique window shapes, Brilliance® pleated shades can be ordered to pull up from the bottom as well as down from the top, allowing for a range of light-filtering possibilities.

In the living room, windows admit light from both east and south. Here, the goals for the window treatments were to preserve the room's clean lines, soften glare from early morning and late afternoon sun, and complement the slipcovered furnishings. Vignette® window shadings in a coordinating "Ballet Slipper" color fit the bill.

This house's privacy requirements change from room to room. Two of the living room windows are relatively small and placed somewhat higher than in other rooms, so privacy isn't as much of an issue. But in the adjacent dining room, *page 107,* the windows form a larger expanse and look directly into the neighbor's lot. The Vignette shadings here stay closed most of the time, providing a translucent privacy screen of filtered light. Beautiful from inside and out, they're a welcome backdrop for family meals and entertaining.

When raised, the living room's Vignette® window shadings in 4-inch folds recede into the headrails, leaving nothing on view but this cottage's old-fashioned charm. When lowered, they provide privacy and reflect warm lamplight.

Two tall-backed, slipcovered chairs in the dining room echo the living room fabrics' colors, and nicely tie the adjacent spaces together. The use of matching-toned Vignette® window shadings in these rooms adds to the pleasing sense of continuity.

In the master bedroom, *pages 108–109,* controlling light took

"Ballet Slipper" Vignette® window shadings in the living room, *opposite,* and dining room, *above,* tie the spaces together and echo the soft edges of the canvas slipcovers and off-white upholstery in both rooms. The shadings also act as privacy screens and turn late daylight into a diffused glow.

precedence over privacy due to an abundance of east-facing windows. Country Woods® wood blinds, with their smooth operation and ability to dial in any amount of light, turned the

Continued on page 110

measuring older windows

Vintage windows are often charmingly detailed, and just as often come with off-kilter frames: These might be wider at the top than the bottom or vice versa. At Hunter Douglas we recommend three key steps to fit treatments to any window.

First, for accuracy, we measure horizontally at top, center, and bottom; vertically at left, center, and right; and diagonally.

Second, for windows that are not square, we generally recommend mounting the headrail on the trim above the window. This way, we can make the shades or blinds about an inch wider than the opening, covering up any light gaps caused by an out-of-square frame. Our headrails are stylish and attractive and cover as little window trim as possible.

Third, if the windowsill slopes, the shade tends to telescope when raising. Many of our shades have adjustable weights in the bottom rail to compensate for this skewing.

When properly measured and fabricated, treatments for older windows can provide as much style, energy efficiency, and privacy as those for newer windows. To get expert help, contact your Hunter Douglas retailer or representative.

now playing: little big rooms

This diminutive cottage employs overscaled furniture and a mostly black-and-white color scheme to produce glamorous interiors worthy of the golden age of cinema. Our feature film starts in the sunroom, *pages 102–103,* where huge potted palms spread their fronds above voluptuous upholstery. In the living room, *pages 104–105,* monumental high-backed armchairs flank a big drum-style library table: You can practically hear movie music throbbing in this space too.

Though it seems illogical that a few imposing furnishings make a small space appear larger, it's true. A room seems to expand to fit its massive contents instead of becoming overwhelmed by a clutter of small things. But since so much is going on with the furniture in this cottage, the window treatments needed to be simple and tailored. Silhouette® window shadings, Vignette® window shadings, Country Woods® wood blinds, and Brilliance® pleated shades provide this house with the perfect restrained backdrop for all its drama.

—*T. Keller Donovan*

Filtering natural light to pleasing effect, Country Woods® wood blinds in "Super White" can be adjusted for light control or opened for an unobstructed view.

Like the kitchen itself, the 2-inch aluminum blinds on the door and window are clean and simple. These treatments in "Dover Suede" with black tapes reinforce the house's color scheme. Plus, the blinds are easy to open and close for sunny views or privacy.

routine of opening the blinds first thing in the morning into a soul-satisfying ritual. As a decorating bonus, the blinds cast bright, graphic patterns of light on the bed linens all morning long.

The kitchen overlooks a short backyard fence, raising privacy issues yet again. Just as important, though, is capitalizing on the light admitted by an over-the-sink window and multipaned door to the deck. White 2-inch aluminum blinds with black tapes address both issues and reiterate the overall color scheme. For the requisite privacy in the bath, a sheer Silhouette® window shading in "Secret Garden" adds a note of color to the vintage architectural details.

Still containing its original tile and sink, the bath, *opposite,* is cozy yet functional. A single Silhouette® window shading provides privacy yet admits diffused light.

surprise in store

This 50-year-old flower shop was remodeled into a studio and living space for an interior designer who wanted a place as unexpected and distinctive as it was functional. The former storefront, which once languished in an inner-city, late-Victorian neighborhood, now presents a strong visual presence to street traffic, while preserving the owner's privacy.

The owner first painted the walls and floors gleaming white and the exposed ceiling trusses lipstick red. In the studio area, an oversize mirror visually enlarges the space—and enhances the drop-dead glamour of the Duette® honeycomb shades in sheer "Black Magic." Clients who come by feel they're in the hands of someone who can find the perfect solution to their decorating dilemmas.

Duette® honeycomb shades open from the top down and the bottom up, so design staffers can review materials in natural light. The high tables are attached to the brick window-wall.

The meeting area, *pages 114–115,* includes a polished rosewood table and plenty of chairs. Here the owner sometimes hosts catered lunches or after-work cocktail parties for clients and favorite suppliers. Shelves along one wall in this area hold a small part of an extensive collection of books on architecture and interior design.

going commercial

Many cities now abate property taxes and offer low-interest rehabilitation loans to welcome entrepreneurs into commercial areas that have seen better days. Such incentives can increase cash flow and help a new business breeze through its difficult early years. As in this case, the business owner may choose to establish a residence within the commercial space too—creating an office-home rather than a home office. That, in turn, creates its own set of light-control and privacy needs—needs that can be stylishly met by creative use of window treatments.

Duette® honeycomb shades in sheer "Black Magic" are ideal for this space, which needs daytime privacy and diffuse natural light. The shades can be adjusted to admit or gently filter the sun—and to reveal or draw a gossamer veil over the view. An added benefit: When lowered, they meld unobtrusively with the linear patterns of the brick walls.

cool, casual, and chic

A pale palette and glossy woodwork make the most of the sunlight that floods this apartment, which occupies a corner of a 30-year-old high rise on the coast of the Atlantic Ocean. Furnished with a mix of antiques and new pieces, the living room is skillfully decorated with a casual sophistication that makes the most of natural textures and beach-inspired earth tones.

Teardrop-shaped louvers give Serenette® SoftFold® Shadings a tailored quality suited to this living room's contemporary furniture and disciplined color scheme. Because they're translucent, these louvers allow in just enough sunshine to create a gentle glow.

Aluminum horizontal blinds control the light in the tiled sunroom. Raised, they maximize the ocean view. As adjusted here, they create the effect of cool, shimmering sheets of water.

With its clean lines and calming color scheme, the apartment called for simple treatments at its generous windows and sliding-glass doors—treatments that also could stand up to the intense ocean-reflected daylight. The softly tailored linen louvers of Serenette® SoftFold® Shadings proved a smart solution.

When they're closed, the overlapping louvers preserve privacy and control light without blocking it entirely, admitting a soft ambient glow. When rotated open, the shadings filter the light; drawn aside, they stack neatly and present an unobstructed view. In addition, the teardrop-shaped louvers of the Serenette shadings provide natural insulation, an important consideration during the region's steamy summer months.

Serenette® SoftFold® Shadings visually unite this dining area with the living room. They also block glare and diffuse the bright daylight, ensuring cool and relaxing mealtimes even in the hottest summer months.

decorating with a neutral palette

Neutral colors—used here in this apartment's living room, sunroom, and dining room—are at once elegant and easy. They present a palette you can live with for years and years. But successfully bringing off such a palette requires a different approach than do other decorating schemes. A neutral room is all about variations in surface and shape: Furnishings, floor coverings, and accessories all contribute to this subtle interplay.

The living room's woven-grass rug grounds the space, *pages 116–117,* with a surface that makes me think of pine needles on a forest floor. Smooth, matte-finished walls contrast with the noticeably textured sofa upholstery (don't miss the important detail of the piping) and the nubby finish of the Serenette® SoftFold® Shadings fabric. A stack of leather-bound books and a massive antique chest with a carved front lend more textures and tones. It's all very quiet, but it will never go out of style—like a great linen suit accented with a string of pearls.

—T. Keller Donovan

Luminette Privacy Sheers® in this sitting room diffuse the strong tropical light and wonderfully echo the soft folds of the curtain panels that frame the room's tall sliding-glass doors. The vanes subtly echo the stripes on the wallpaper as well. A green-and-white fern-printed cotton fabric unifies the curtains, armless side chair, ruffle-skirted sofa, and pillows. A paler green was chosen for the wallpaper stripes, visually increasing the sitting room's height and providing a crisp background for treasured, flower-strewn pieces of heirloom china.

The wood furniture here is uniformly dark, emphasizing form and shape over potentially disruptive color. A white-painted wall bracket and white porcelain cask used as a side table strike cooling notes. The rattan-wrapped mirror frame and picture frames further evoke the region's equatorial climate. Thanks to its simplicity and restraint, this sitting room manages to achieve a relaxed yet tailored composure. The Luminette Privacy Sheers certainly contribute to this mood: As they diffuse the natural light, they create a gentle overall glow that pulls together the room's varied textures and materials.

decorating with light

Sometimes a window treatment's biggest contribution to a decorating scheme is the quality of light it admits. Luminette Privacy Sheers®, *right,* screen plain sliding-glass doors with a gauzy scrim of light-filtering fabric. The result is similar to that produced by a portrait photographer's "soft box": an even, almost shadowless light that flatters everything it touches. The diffused light also helps visually unify diverse patterns and surfaces, such as the fern print, stripes, and rattan shown here.

Resembling rice-paper blinds, Silhouette® window shadings in "White" extend this master bedroom's Asian decorating theme. A whimsical blue-and-white cotton toile covers a curvaceous sofa and tall folding screen, and forms the bed's dust ruffle. Framed prints of antique porcelains nicely echo the Chinese garden seat—used here as a side table—and the ginger-jar lamp base. By softening the sunlight, the Silhouette window shadings wonderfully accentuate this bedroom's dreamy ambience.

Horizontal blinds and translucent fabric curtain panels give a safari-tent air to this bedroom. Wildlife prints, faux-animal-skin accents, an oversize tropical plant, and ticking-striped twin beds continue the theme. A pith helmet and an antique-map lampshade add finishing touches to the room, which was planned to encourage weekend visitors' imaginations and wanderlust.

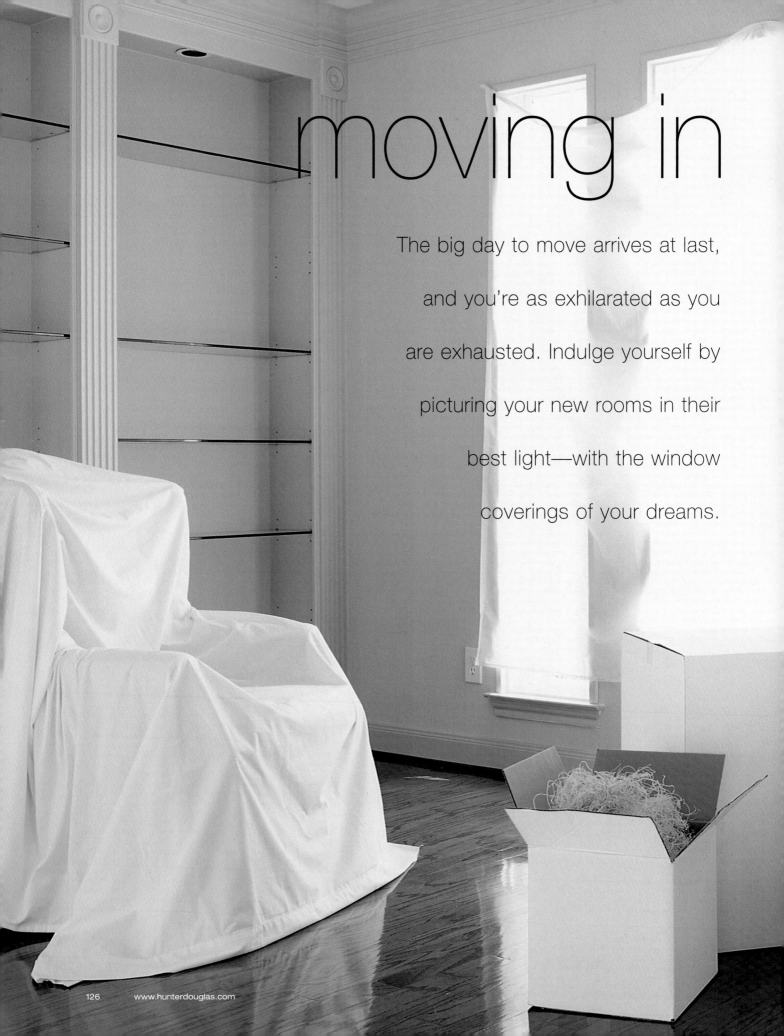

moving in

The big day to move arrives at last,

and you're as exhilarated as you

are exhausted. Indulge yourself by

picturing your new rooms in their

best light—with the window

coverings of your dreams.

A new house always holds great promise: It's the place where you'll nurture your family, entertain friends, and soothe your soul. For every room of your new house, you want the perfect mix of style, comfort, and practicality. And nowhere is this mix more important than at your windows. Depending on how they're oriented, they can admit full sun or diffuse daylight. Windows also provide opportunities to enhance the look and function of your rooms.

When you plan your window treatments, consider first: "How will we use this room? What activities do we need to think about?" If you're moving into a newly built house, you can start the decision-making process as soon as the walls and window openings are framed.

"Have a master plan," says New York City interior designer T. Keller Donovan. "If you determine the overall decorating scheme for each room up front, you can zero in on the details that make a big difference—the color of your pleated shades, for example, or whether or not you'll want tapes for your wood blinds." Donovan encourages his clients to consider a wide palette for their window coverings: "Neutrals are always safe for any room you're going to spend a lot of time in, but it's fun to try a blast of color in a powder room or dining room."

Privacy and decorative appeal probably are the first things that occur to you. But consider energy efficiency, ultraviolet-light protection, and sound absorption, too. Window coverings can do much to keep your rooms comfortably cool or warm, protect fabrics from damaging sun, and modulate outside noise. "Spend some time in each room," Donovan suggests, "so you can see, for instance, how light moves through the space during the course of a day." As you walk through your new house, consider the following room-specific issues.

Living, dining, and family rooms: A living room with an entertainment center needs light-blocking treatments that minimize glare when your family gathers to watch a favorite movie. In the dining room, you're more likely to want light-diffusing treatments that provide privacy, soft illumination, and a touch of elegance for entertaining. Family rooms often are in use around the clock, so treatments here should be versatile enough to allow light control during the day and privacy at night—and be simple to adjust.

Kitchen: No surprise here—the hardest-working room also demands hard-working window treatments. Light control is essential, but so is ventilation. Consider coverings that allow cooling breezes to enter and heat to escape even as they provide varying levels of privacy. Also be sure they stand up to heat and humidity and are easy to clean.

Bath: Your first priority is privacy, but bath treatments also need to withstand near-constant humidity. For an area near a tub, shower, or spa, consider composite Palm Beach™ shutters, which won't warp, crack, or mildew. Shades that open from the top down are also popular. They admit light and allow heat and humidity to escape while covering the lower part of the window for privacy.

Master bedroom: Privacy is key here, too. But so is enjoying the

view and controlling light. Do you want to be greeted by a glimmer of sunlight every morning or awaken to a darkened room? Is there a view you'd like to enhance or obscure? Play up architectural details with wood blinds or shutters or create a voluptuous air with soft honeycomb or pleated shades.

Children's rooms: Because nothing is more important to you than your children's safety, kids' rooms are perfect places to take advantage of the new cordless LiteRise® hardware from Hunter Douglas. Also consider bright shade colors to please youngsters.

Home office: Here it's especially important to maximize daylight but also to be able to control it. You'll need diffuse, nonglare illumination to avoid reflections off the computer monitor; bright light for reading or working with color; and cheerful general illumination for client meetings.

Throughout the house, you'll want to use the newest Hunter Douglas innovations in window hardware: The LiteRise® Touch System, which eliminates the need for cords; UltraGlide™, with a retractable cord that stays at a constant length; and PowerRise® for remote-control operating ease. There's even a home-automation system that integrates control of natural light

Raw-silk Jubilance® Roman shades screen these living room windows from passersby and complement the eclectic decor. The "Cypress" color echoes that of the slipcovered wing chairs.

with your house's artificial light so you can create just the right balance from a single control.

Visit your local Hunter Douglas dealer early in your moving-in process and explore all of your window treatment options. Call 800-937-7895 or visit www.hunterdouglas.com to find the dealer nearest you. A lifetime of style, comfort, and function awaits.

tips for measuring

To ensure your new treatments are a perfect fit, follow our easy steps.
1. Decide whether your window covering will be mounted outside or inside the window opening.
2. To take all measurements, use a steel measuring tape. Rulers and cloth tapes may not give you accurate results.
3. For outside mounting:
   - Width measurement: Measure from one outside edge of the window casing to the other. Add at least 3 inches (1½ inches on each side) to eliminate possible light gaps.
   - Height measurement: Measure from the lowest point to the highest point you'd like your window treatment to cover.
4. For inside mounting:
   - Width measurement: Measure across the window opening from one inside edge to the other. Measure in three places and use the narrowest measurement.
   - Height measurement: Measure from the top inside edge of the window opening to the top of the sill.

If you're not confident about your measuring skills, let your local Hunter Douglas dealer measure your windows for you.

one family room, a trio of treatments

The arched windows in many new family rooms look good dressed in a number of Hunter Douglas products. Here are three stylish looks for a typical space.

Country Woods® Classics™ 2-inch wood blinds in "Ranch Oak" add a crisp, clean architectural air to the room—and afford maximum light control. Angling the slats up directs light at the ceiling, providing even, glare-free illumination. These blinds also feature de-Light™, an option that eliminates visible cord-routing holes, blocking even pinhole rays of light when closed.

"Straw" Serenette® SoftFold™ Shadings lend a textured-linen look. Shirred matching fabric in the window's arch provides a custom touch. Serenette shadings have teardrop-shaped louvers that allow for an unobstructed view, varying degrees of translucent light, or total privacy.

The straightforward, casual-contemporary feel of these "Spring Green" Duette® honeycomb shades complements the furnishings even as the shades protect them from the sun. The honeycomb construction traps an insulating layer of air inside the shade to block drafts and minimize heat loss. The treatment's Easy View® Arch can be lowered from the top to permit more sunlight into the room.

Translucent Luminette Privacy Sheers® enhance the pale, cloud-like quality of this bedroom and nicely complement the gentle folds of the curtains they're paired with. They also effectively reduce the glaring light reflected off a backyard swimming pool. For more information on this treatment, see *page 135*.

Hunter Douglas
product guide

Use our handy guide to learn even more about the window treatments we've featured in this book.

Aluminum Horizontal Blinds *left:* Available in many colors, these blinds complement a range of decors. They also provide complete light control at an affordable price. The slats come in solid-color, metallic, hammered, brushed, pearlescent, leather-like SoftSuede®, and linen-like Softweave™ finishes and in micro blind ½-inch, conventional 1-inch, and bold 2-inch widths.

Lightlines® Mini Blinds *(shown on page 72):* These elegant ½-inch aluminum horizontal blinds feature the de-Light™ option that eliminates unwanted light leaks that interrupt sleep, fade furnishings, and cause glare. The blinds blend the valance, headrail, and slats into a sleek overall look. The slats are treated with the exclusive Dust Shield™ coating to reduce dust build-up. They are also heat-treated for extra "bounce-back" resilience.

Care and maintenance: Dust aluminum horizontal blinds and Lightlines mini blinds with a feather duster or cloth, or vacuum with a brush attachment. Treat stains immediately with a household spray cleaner. Wash annually in a tub of warm soapy water.

Break-Thru® Safety Tassels: These fracture-resistant tassels have a break-apart feature to protect children and pets from injury. They can be installed on aluminum horizontal blinds and Country Woods® wood blinds.

Brilliance® Pleated Shades *right and above right:* With their crisp, pleated fabrics in hundreds of colors and their color-

Country Woods® Wood Blinds *left and right:* These horizontal wood blinds exude tradition and character. The warm wood tones enhance any room, be it a bookcase-lined home office, a country kitchen, or a tailored bedroom. Available in many colors and woods, they feature classically proportioned 2-inch slats or 1-inch slats for smaller windows. They provide complete light control and can be customized with fabric tapes and accent trims. The Country Woods Collection includes these distinctive models:

Reflections™: 2⅝-inch beveled basswood slats in 14 stock colors and custom hues.

Select™: 1-inch or 2-inch slats in genuine oak, honey oak, cherry, and maple.

Classics™: 1-inch or 2-inch basswood slats stained or painted in 27 stock colors and custom hues.

Care and maintenance: Dust with a feather duster or cloth, vacuum with a brush attachment, or use spray cans of compressed air (available at office-supply, hardware, and grocery stores).

de-Light™: This exclusive feature eliminates the light leaks that can enter through connecting-cord holes. It's an option on Lightlines® mini blinds and Country Woods wood blinds.

Duette® Honeycomb Shades *right and page 136, top left,* with PowerRise®: These shades come in

coordinated hardware, these shades provide complete light control and privacy when lowered and a full window view when raised. They also help insulate glass, increasing a window's R-value (resistance to heat loss) by as much as 70 percent and blocking 60–90 percent of ultraviolet light.

Care and maintenance: Dust with a feather duster or cloth, vacuum with a brush attachment, or use spray cans of compressed air (available at office-supply, hardware, and grocery stores). Ask your dealer if professional ultrasonic cleaning is suitable for your fabric.

hundreds of colors and in sheer, semiopaque, and opaque fabrics. They control light, increase window-insulation values by 25–175 percent (depending on whether single, double, or triple honeycombs are used), block 99 percent of the sun's ultraviolet rays, and increase sound absorption. The single-honeycomb shade comes in ½-inch, ⅜-inch, ¾-inch, and 1-inch pleats and is great for customizing to fit arches and unusually shaped windows.

Care and maintenance: Dust with a feather duster or cloth, vacuum with a brush attachment, or use spray cans of compressed air (available at office-supply, hardware, and grocery stores). Ask your dealer if professional ultrasonic cleaning is suitable for your fabric.

Duette® honeycomb shades are available with the following options and features, making them even more versatile and practical. The care and mainte-nance for all the options are the same as for the Duette honeycomb shades.

Duette Duolite® Shades *left:* These ingenious treatments allow you to combine two fabrics of different opacities in the same shade, letting in varying degrees of filtered light and creating privacy at the same time. Choose from sheer, semisheer, semiopaque, and opaque fabrics.

Duette Vertiglide® Shades *below:* These treatments have the same Duette honeycomb construction but are hung with the pleats oriented vertically. Perfect for sliding-glass and French doors, they can be installed to draw to either side, both sides, or the center. The treatment's ¾-inch pleat can be ordered in sheer, semiopaque, and

opaque fabrics. No matter how wide their expanse, these shades always stack to a discreet 6 inches.

Duette® with Ultraglide™ Shades: These shades feature a retractable-cord system that keeps the cord length the same when adjusting the shades. This system keeps the cords out of the reach of children for maximum safety.

Easy Rise™: This looped cord system makes adjusting larger window shades easier. It's an option on Duette® honeycomb shades with ¾-inch pleats.

Everwood® Alternative Wood Blinds *above:* Made of a blend of hardwoods and composite materials,

these blinds have extra resistance to fading, warping, and cracking—welcome attributes in hot, humid rooms like the kitchen and bath. The 2-inch slats come in 20 colors and textured "etched" finishes that resemble hand-carved wood; all can be customized with decorative tapes. A 2⅝-inch beveled slat provides tighter closure and better views when open.

Care and maintenance: Dust with a feather duster or cloth, vacuum with a brush attachment, or spot-clean with household spray cleaner.

Jubilance® Roman Shades *right and bottom left:* Like a chameleon, these shades can change their appearance, depending on which of the many fabrics you choose— from elegant raw silk to casual grasslike cloth. The fabric stacks in 10-inch panels when they're raised; lowered, the shades exhibit a smart tailored look and provide privacy. Jubilance shades are an affordable choice for maximum light control and a 14-percent increase in energy efficiency. An attached valance conceals the headrail and shade when raised, so the covering seems to disappear when not in use.

Care and maintenance: Dust with a feather duster or cloth, vacuum with a brush attachment, or spot-clean with a household spray cleaner.

LiteRise® Touch System: This feature, *right,* lets you raise and lower your window treatments with the touch of a fin-

ger, increasing safety and convenience. It's available on Brilliance® pleated shades, Country Woods® wood blinds, Duette® honeycomb shades, and 1-inch Decor® aluminum blinds.

Luminette Privacy Sheers® *above and below left:* Soft fabric vanes attached to translucent facings combine the look of a sheer curtain with superior light control and privacy. The polyester fabric comes in neutrals and pastels. When the vanes are closed, the sheers block 55–99 percent of UV light and increase window insulation values 31–43 percent. Especially suited for larger, rectangular windows, the sheers can be effectively paired with Silhouette® window shadings for mixing horizontal and vertical applications.

Care and maintenance: Dust with a feather duster or cloth, or vacuum with a brush attachment.

Palm Beach™ Custom Shutters *below:* Made of a polymer compound that won't warp, crack, chip, or shrink, these versatile shutters come in white and off-white finishes. The slats also are treated with Dust Shield™ coating system and are heat-treated for extra resiliency. They're especially good for difficult-to-dress bay or clerestory windows and are appropriate for any room in the house. Choose from 2⅜-inch or 3⅜-inch louver sizes in Palmetto™ or Lantana™ styles. Palmetto shutters have a traditional tilt bar to adjust the louvers. Lantana shutters allow you to open and close all louvers at once with the touch of a finger. Both styles give you the installation options of a standard hinged system, a bifold track, or a bi-

pass track that lets the shutters slide open and shut.

Care and maintenance: Dust with a feather duster or cloth, vacuum with a brush attachment, or use spray cans of compressed air (available at office-supply, hardware, and grocery stores). Clean spots immediately with mild soap and water.

PowerRise® Battery-Operated Remote-Control System

above left (shown with Duette® honeycomb shades): This system works via an infrared sensor on the headrail to let you raise and lower your shades and blinds with the press of a button. It has a memory stop that allows for automatic raising to any level you desire. It's available on Brilliance® pleated shades, Duette® honeycomb shades, and Silhouette® window shadings.

Provenance™ Woven Wood Shades

right: Made of fine wood and natural bamboo, these shades are uniquely textured, adding casual good looks to any room. When lowered, the shades lie flat; when raised, they hang in even, overlap-

ping folds. They're available in a rich assortment of bamboo, reeds, slats, and grasses. An attached decorative valance is standard. These exceptionally durable shades are available with several important options: They can be fabricated for easy top-down/bottom-up operation; specialty angle-top shades can be designed for windows with a sloped top; for banks of windows, the shades are available with side-by-side shades on one headrail; for extra opacity, you can add a fabric liner or micro-pleat shade, which will block 98 percent of a room's light and ensure complete privacy.

Care and maintenance: Dust with a feather duster or cloth, vacuum with a brush attachment, or use

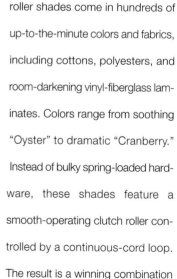

spray cans of compressed air (available at office-supply, hardware, and grocery stores).

Remembrance® Window Shades

opposite, top left: These traditional roller shades come in hundreds of up-to-the-minute colors and fabrics, including cottons, polyesters, and room-darkening vinyl-fiberglass laminates. Colors range from soothing "Oyster" to dramatic "Cranberry." Instead of bulky spring-loaded hardware, these shades feature a smooth-operating clutch roller controlled by a continuous-cord loop. The result is a winning combination of light control, privacy, and a 16–43 percent increase in window insulating value. A range of decorative hems and trims lets you indulge your personal style and customize your shades.

Care and maintenance: Dust with a feather duster or cloth, vacuum with a brush attachment, or spot-clean using a household spray cleaner that's appropriate for your fabric.

Serenette® SoftFold® Shadings *right:* These elegant fabric window shadings combine the appearance of tailored draperies with engineering innovations that allow them to function like vertical blinds for better light control. By rotating the wand cord tensioner, you can adjust the 4¼-inch teardrop-shaped fabric louvers, *left,* for total light control and privacy. The wand is also a safety feature. Choose from 50 neutral colors available in eight fabrics, including translucent "Lace," room-darkening "Nocturne Crepe," and fashionable "Linen," "Damask," and "Taffeta." Enhance your shadings with a custom overtreatment in a matching Serenette fabric, available by the yard.

Care and maintenance: Ask your Hunter Douglas dealer about professional ultrasonic cleaning.

Silhouette® Window Shadings *top right and page 138, top left:* These versatile shadings suspend

fabric vanes between two sheer fabric facings. The suspended vanes tilt the way more traditional horizontal blinds do, allowing you total light control for everything from a filtered view to complete privacy. When raised the shading completely disappears into the headrail for an unobstructed view. Choose 2- or 3-inch vanes in a variety of fabrics, colors, and facings. Or opt for Nantucket™ window shadings for an informal look.

particularly well in rooms with contemporary furnishings and are the perfect design solution for unifying sliding-glass patio doors.

Care and maintenance: Dust with a feather duster or cloth, vacuum with a brush attachment, or use spray cans of compressed air (available at office-supply, hardware, and grocery stores). Vinyl and aluminum blinds also may be spot-cleaned with a household spray cleaner.

Vignette® Window Shadings *opposite, top left and opposite left:* Featuring gentle folds of fabric that measure 3 or 4 inches wide, Vignette shadings let you coordinate your treatments with your decor. The

look. They feature 2½-inch vanes and fabric colors inspired by sea, sand, and sky.

Care and maintenance: Dust with a feather duster or cloth, vacuum with a brush attachment, or use spray cans of compressed air (available at office-supply, hardware, and grocery stores). Or engage the services of a professional for ultrasonic cleaning; consult your Hunter Douglas dealer for details on your particular fabric.

Vertical Blinds *right:* Whether they're made of fabric, vinyl, or aluminum, vertical blinds offer complete light control, block 95–99 percent of ultraviolet light, and increase a window's insulation value by 37–123 percent. Hunter Douglas® vertical blinds feature 3½-inch vanes in hundreds of colors, textures, and embossed patterns. They work

consult your Hunter Douglas dealer for details on your fabric.

Woodmates® Alternative Wood Blinds *below:* These horizontal blinds capture the look of real wood but are made entirely of polymer compounds that won't fade, warp, or crack. Their 2-inch slats come in a number of colors and textures.

Care and maintenance: Regularly dust with a feather duster or cloth, or vacuum with a brush attachment. Spot-clean using warm soapy water or a household spray cleaner.

Call Hunter Douglas at 1-800-937-7895 for more information or to find a dealer near you.

shading combines the classic look of a custom curtain with the ease of a shade. More than 100 colors and a wide range of fabrics are available. When lowered, they block 99 percent of ultraviolet rays and increase window insulation values by 49 percent. When raised the shading completely disappears into the headrail for an unobstructed view.

Care and maintenance: Dust with a feather duster or cloth, vacuum with a brush attachment, or use spray cans of compressed air (available at office-supply, hardware, and grocery stores). Or engage the services of a professional for ultrasonic cleaning;

Professionals Directory

Photographers

Pages 2, 16, 24-33, 42-45, 46-49, 56-63, 82-85, 92-101, 133 (bottom right)
Fran Brennan
Fran Brennan Photography
2337 Tangley Road
Houston, TX 77005
Phone: 713-526-9206

Pages 1, 10-15 (courtesy of *House Beautiful*), 18-19, 116-125, 135 (bottom right)
Carlos Domenech
Carlos Domenech Photography
6060 SW. 26th Street
Miami, FL 33155
Phone: 305-666-6964

Pages 8, 20-23, 38-41, 137
Colleen Duffley
Colleen Duffley Photography
3303 Lee Parkway, Suite 101
Dallas, TX 75219
Phone: 214-520-9675
Fax: 214-520-9515

Pages 6-7, 50-55, 64-67, 68-81, 86-91, 92-101, 102-111, 126-129, 131, 133 (top left), 138 (top left), 139 (both), 144
Susan Gilmore
Susan Gilmore Photography
8415 Wesley Drive
Minneapolis, MN 55427
Phone: 612-545-4608
Fax: 612-545-2693

Pages 5, 34-37, 68-81, 112-115, 126-129, 130, 132, 134 (both), 135 (top left), 136, 140
Brad Simmons
Brad Simmons Photography
870 Craintown Road
Perryville, KY 40568
Phone: 858-332-8400
Fax: 859-332-4433
Web site:
www.bradsimmons.com

Interior Designers

Pages 132, 133 (top left), 134 (top left), 139 (bottom right), 144
Ginger Barber
Ginger Barber Design, Inc., and The Sitting Room
2402 Quenby
Houston, TX 77005
Phone: 713-523-1925
Fax: 713-523-1929
Web site: www.thesittingroom.net

Pages 38-41, 137
Kimber Cavendish, F²C

300 Academy
Austin, TX 78704
Phone: 512-912-9500

Pages 92-101, 126-129, 134 (bottom left), 138 (top left)
Cathy Chapman
Chapman Design, Inc.
7026 Old Katy Road, Suite 163A
Houston, TX 77024
Phone: 713-864-8622 (office)
Phone: 713-202-9219 (cell)

Pages 130, 135 (top left), 136
Trisha Dodson
Trisha Dodson Interiors
725 Riedel
Houston, TX 77024
Phone: 713-973-6802
E-mail:
trisha_dodson@hotmail.com

Pages 1, 10-15, 18-19, 116-125, 135 (bottom right)
T. Keller Donovan
Keller Donovan, Inc.
325 W. 38th St., Suite 1101
New York, NY 10018
Phone: 212-760-0537
Fax: 212-760-0596
E-mail: tkellerd@aol.com

Pages 64-67
Eccentricities
1921 Westheimer
Houston, TX 77098
Phone: 713-523-1921
Fax: 713-523-3993

Pages 2, 24-33, 42-45, 56-63, 86-91, 112-115, 133 (bottom right)
Richard Holley
Richard Holley Design
3412 Audubon Place
Houston, TX 77006
Phone: 713-524-0066
Fax: 713-524-5659
E-mail: studiorh@flash.net

Pages 5, 34-37
Jerry Jeanmard
Wells Design/Jerry Jeanmard
2121 San Felipe
Houston, TX 77019
Phone: 713-526-8200
Fax: 713-526-8913
E-mail: wellsjj@swbell.net

Pages 68-81, 139 (top left), 140
Margaret Mohr
John Kidd Associates
5120 Woodway, Suite 7033
Houston, TX 77056
Phone: 713-961-1888
Fax: 713-961-1912

Pages 50-55, 131
Marlys Tokerud
Tokerud & Co. Interior Design
4606 Greenbriar
Houston, TX 77005-6862
Phone: 713-520-8666
Fax: 713-529-1960

Pages 20-23
Susan Castor Wilson, ASID
The Castor Collection
3820 Alameda, Suite 38
Corpus Christi, TX 78411
Phone: 361-851-8052
Fax: 361-851-8017
E-mail:
susan@castorcollection.com
Web site:
www.castorcollection.com

Pages 6-7, 102-111
Liz Zamadics
Hestia Design
1955 Norfolk
Houston, TX 77098
Phone: 713-523-1857

Architects

Pages 42-45
Colby Design
602 Harold
Houston, TX 77006
Phone: 713-524-1497
Fax: 713-524-1340

Pages 8, 38-41, 137
Richard deVarga
Mallet deVarga
1905A S. First Street
Austin, TX 78704
Phone: 512-444-8902
Fax: 512-444-8962
E-mail: rdevargas@aol.com

Pages 16, 82-85
Dillon Kyle
Dillon Kyle Architecture, Inc.
3219 Milam
Houston, TX 77005
Phone: 713-520-8792
Fax: 713-520-9635
E-mail: dillonkyle@dkarc.com
Web site: www.dkarc.com

Pages 20-23
Ignacio Salas-Humara, AIA
P.O. Box 158
Comfort, TX 78103
Phone: 830-995-4217
Fax: 830-995-3577
E-mail: salas@hctc.net

Pages 2, 24-33
Joe Williams
Houston, TX
Phone: 713-524-2468

Builders

Pages 16, 82-85
Hahnseld Witmer Davis Builders, Inc.
3100 Alabama Ct.
Houston, TX 77027
Phone: 713-840-7178
Fax: 713-840-7177
Web site: www.hwdinc.com

Pages 126-129, 134 (bottom left)
McGuyer Homebuilders, Inc./Coventry Homes (model home at Gleannloch Farms)
1315 Richlawn
Spring, TX 77379
Susan Fendley (marketing representative)
Phone: 713-952-6767

Pages 92-101
Southampton Group, Inc.
2472 Bolsover Road, Suite 371
Houston, TX 77005
Phone: 713-528-0264
Fax: 713-528-0263
E-mail: mbarone@flash.net

Pages 56-63, 133 (bottom right)
Landscape architect Steve Henry
Gregory Henry Landscapes, Inc.
1219 Durham Drive
Houston, TX 77007
Phone: 713-426-3311
Fax: 713-426-3639

Pages 68-81
Master carpenter Mike Little
3106 Nottingham
Houston, TX 77005
Phone: 713-666-5846

Photo Stylists

Pages 1, 10-15, 18-19, 116-125
T. Keller Donovan
(See Interior Designers)

Pages 68-81, 126-129
Joetta Moulden
www.shelterstyle.com
P.O. Box 9337-B
Katy Freeway #176
Houston, TX 77024
Phone: 713-461-2063 (office)
Phone: 713-829-1887 (cell)

Pages 8, 20-23, 38-41
Helen Thompson
Phone: 512-477-0920

Field Editors

Pages 2, 5, 16, 24-33, 34-37, 42-45, 56-63, 64-67, 82-85, 86-91, 112-115
Fran Brennan
(see Photographers)

Pages 1, 10-15, 18-19, 116-125
T. Keller Donovan
(see Interior Designers)

Pages 6-7, 46-49, 50-55, 68-81, 92-101, 102-111, 126-129
Joetta Moulden
(see Photo Stylists)

Pages 8, 20-23, 38-41
Helen Thompson
(see Photo Stylists)

Tapestria™

In a number of houses in this book, fabrics were used from a new Hunter Douglas service called Tapestria™. This online market enables interior design companies to obtain fabrics directly from more than 40 of Europe's leading mills. From the Web site, *www.Tapestria.com*, designers can search, view, and order free fabric samples, check and reserve inventory, and place and track orders with confidence, convenience, and speed.

Fabrics in the following photos in this book were obtained through Tapestria.
Page 22: sofa slipcovers and pillows
Page 28: tablecloth
Page 56: bench cushions
Page 59: sofa pillows
Page 61: pillows on chaise
Page 62: headboard
Pages 70-73: table skirt
Page 91: sofa pillows
Pages 94-95: sofa pillows and curtains
Pages 96-97: curtains
Pages 100-101: curtains
Pages 102-103: pillows
Pages 104-106: pillows
Page 107: tablecloth
Pages 108-109: pillows
Page 133: bench cushions
Page 135 (top left): valance and sofa pillows
Page 138 (top left): valance and pillows
Pages 139 (bottom right) and 144: curtains

Luminette Privacy Sheers®, *opposite*, allow diffused views. Visual warmth and a traditional look are supplied by Everwood® alternative wood blinds, *page 144*.